JEWISH HOLIDAY FEASTS

BY LOUISE FISZER & JEANNETTE FERRARY

ILLUSTRATIONS BY COCO MASUDA

CHRONICLE BOOKS

SAN FRANCISCO

DEDICATION

To Bella and Ethel,
To Loretta and Bessie,
and to Jewish mothers everywhere regardless
of race, creed, sex, or place of national origin.

This hardcover edition published by Chronicle Books LLC in 2005.

Text copyright © 1995 by Louise Fiszer and Jeannette Ferrary.
Illustrations copyright © 1995 by Coco Masuda.

ISBN 0-8118-5045-5

The Library of Congress has cataloged the previous edition as follows:

Ferrary, Jeannette, 1941 –
        Jewish holiday feasts / by Jeannette Ferrary, Louise Fiszer.
                    p.   cm.
        Includes index.
        ISBN 0-8118-0704-5
        1. cookery, Jewish. 2. Holiday cookery.
        3. Cookery—Religious aspects—Judaism.
        4. Fasts and feasts—Judaism. I. Fiszer, Louise. II. Title.
        TX724.F377 1995
        641.5'676—dc20   94-43518
                                                          CIP

Manufactured in China.

Cover Design by Tim Belonax
Interior Design by Deborah Bowman
Typesetting by Deborah Bowman

Distributed in Canada by Raincoast Books
9050 Shaughnessy Street
Vancouver, British Columbia V6P 6E5

10 9 8 7 6 5 4 3 2 1

Chronicle Books LLC
85 Second Street
San Francisco, California 94105

www.chroniclebooks.com

CONTENTS

INTRODUCTION
6

AUTUMN

ROSH HASHANAH
8

Persimmon and Pomegranate Salad
Round Raisin Challah
Honey & Cumin-Glazed Cornish Hens
Couscous with Saffron and Vegetables
Braised Apples and Red Cabbage with Wine
Hannah's Honey Cake

YOM KIPPUR
16

Fresh Vegetable Soup with Chicken and Noodles
Toasted Bagels with Eggplant Spread
Spiced Pear and Almond Cake

SUCCOTH
20

Sweet and Hot Pepper Tomato Soup with Mint
Pita Stuffed with Eggplant Salad and Feta Cheese
Fennel, Cucumber, and Orange Salad
Baked Figs with Honeyed Yogurt

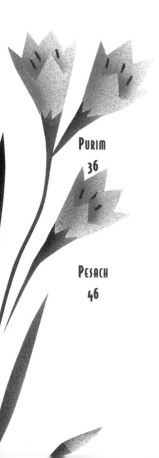

HANUKKAH
26

Spinach Salad with Tangerines and Dried Cranberries

Classic Potato Latkes

Zucchini Latkes

Fresh Salmon Latkes

Cauliflower and Carrot Latkes

Sweet Cottage Cheese Latkes with Apple-Pear Puree

SPRING

PURIM
36

Hamantashen with Prune Filling

Hamantashen with Fig Filling

Walnut and Dried Cherry Rugelach

Apricot-Almond-Chocolate Balls

Chocolate-Orange Squares

PESACH
46

Carrot-Matzo Ball Soup

Rolled Turkey Breast with Mushroom-Spinach Stuffing

Asparagus with Orange Vinaigrette

Dried Cherry and Pear Haroset

Sweet-Potato Kugel

Passover Biscotti

SUMMER

SHAVUOTH
56

Cold Beet and Cucumber Soup

Asparagus and Herbed Cheese Strudel

Poached Salmon with Two Sauces

Lemon-Mustard Sauce

Roasted Tomato and Red Pepper Sauce

Very Berry Blintzes with Berry Sauce

YEAR ROUND

FOODS OF THE SABBATH
64

Golden Challah Bread

Tomato and Onion Braised Brisket

Roasted Garlic Potato Wedges

Sugar Snap Peas and Honeyed Carrots

Strawberry, Pineapple, and Mango Compote

71   INDEX

72   TABLE OF EQUIVALENTS

INTRODUCTION

"**D**on't do anything too weird," a traditional Jewish cook advised us as we began this book. "I like new ideas, but I also like going back every year to my comfortable old recipes. Nobody wants to be eating experiments, especially on the High Holy Days." ✳ She was right, of course. And we felt pretty much the same way. We wanted to make a nice little book that would have everything: recipes that conform to the requirements of the holiday, that meet the expectations of traditional taste, that preserve the richness and meaning of the beloved customary foods. We wanted to do them in a light style with fresh, flavorful ingredients tailored to today's health-conscious needs. Simple but interesting; not boring but not difficult or intimidating either. ✳ We tasted and tested and researched traditional Jewish holiday foods from every part of the world–from Russia, Spain, and Greece to Israel, Latin America, and Eastern Europe. Among the differences, we found an amazing consistency in the way these dishes reflect the land they are from, their time of year. They all, in some way, honor the wisdom of the earth: winter's sleep, spring's awakening, the cornucopia of summer, the autumn harvest. The feasts and festivals of the Jewish calendar, which together tell the sacred story of a people, are tied to the cycles of nature, its demands and generosities. That is why we decided to arrange the book by season and to cook with foods and ingredients that eloquently reflect that hallowed bond. "These are the feasts of the Lord," announces Leviticus 23:4, "which ye shall proclaim in their seasons." ✳ We introduce each holiday with some background information about its history and meaning. Wherever possible, we include explanations about how each dish fits into the tradition and why it is served. ✳ Finally, because today's cook almost always enjoys limited time in the kitchen, all recipes are straightforward and quickly prepared. We hope you will find this a concise and complete one-stop helper for every holiday: easy to use, exciting to cook from and, most of all, not too weird.

LESHANA TOVA TIKOSEVU–May you be inscribed for a good year–is the familiar greeting of Rosh Hashanah, the high holy days that begin the Jewish new year. A time of reflection and resolution, Rosh Hashanah is also a time of joy and hope for the year to come. The holiday begins on the first of Tishre, which falls in late September or early October, and continues through the Ten Days of Awe, or Days of Penitence, until Yom Kippur, the Day of Atonement. This ancient holiday time resonates with much of the modern world which, at this time of year, has returned from summer retreats to begin the new season: at school and college, in business, in the fields, and with friends and family as the social calendar gets under way. ✳ Rosh Hashanah is known under many names, each underscoring a different aspect of the holy days' significance. As *Yom ha-Din,* or the Day of Judgment, this is a time of examination, evaluation, and repentance. As *Yom ha-Zikaron,* the Day of Remembrance, it refers to the eternity of time and the continuity of past and present. As *Yom Teruah,* or the Day of the Blowing of the Horn, it recalls the *shofar,* or ram's horn, which is sounded during the religious services as a reminder of spiritual awakening. ✳ On Rosh Hashanah, special additions to the dinner table include the season's new fruits, like pomegranates, avocados and persimmons, a plate of sliced apples or bread, and a pot of honey for dipping. These signify hope for a sweet year ahead and are eaten with the accompanying prayer: "May it be Thy will, Oh Lord our God, to renew unto us a happy and pleasant new year."

9

PERSIMMON AND POMEGRANATE SALAD

Serves 8

One of the gustatory joys of Rosh Hashanah is the introduction of fruits not commonly enjoyed by the family. This salad offers two of them in a slightly sweet and sour combination meant also to represent the wish for fruitfulness and plenty in the new year. The Fuyu is the preferred persimmon in this salad because of its crisp texture.

> 8 cups torn spinach leaves or other seasonal greens, (about 1 pound)
> 3 Fuyu persimmons, cut into thin wedges
> 1 small red onion, thinly sliced
> 3 tablespoons sherry vinegar
> 7 tablespoons olive oil
> Salt and pepper
> Seeds from 1 large pomegranate
>   (about 1 cup)

IN A LARGE BOWL, COMBINE SPINACH, PERSIMMONS, AND ONION. Whisk together vinegar and oil. Toss with salad. Add salt and pepper to taste. Sprinkle with pomegranate seeds and serve.

ROUND RAISIN CHALLAH

Makes 1 loaf

During Rosh Hashanah, challah is often shaped into forms other than the usual braid. It may look like wings to associate man with the angels or like a ladder to facilitate our prayers reaching heaven. As a round form such as this one, the challah recalls the crown of God's kingdom or the circle of life.

2 packages dry yeast	*¼ cup sugar*
⅛ teaspoon saffron threads	*2 teaspoons salt*
⅔ cups warm water (about 110 degrees F.)	*4½ to 5 cups all-purpose flour*
5 egg yolks, lightly beaten	*1½ cups raisins*
3 eggs, lightly beaten	*1 egg yolk, beaten*
7 tablespoons vegetable or canola oil	

IN A LARGE BOWL, SOAK YEAST AND SAFFRON IN WATER ABOUT 5 MINUTES. Stir in egg yolks, eggs, oil, sugar, and salt. Add enough flour to form a stiff but sticky dough, about 4½ cups. Turn dough out on floured surface and knead until smooth and elastic, about 6 minutes, working raisins in dough while kneading. Form into a ball and place in a greased bowl. Turn dough to grease entire surface. Cover with plastic wrap and place in a warm spot until doubled in bulk, about 2 hours.

Punch down dough and knead briefly. Roll dough into a rope about 24 inches long. Coil rope into a spiral round loaf. Place on a greased cookie sheet. Brush with beaten yolk and let rise in warm place until doubled, about 45 minutes.

Preheat the oven to 375 degrees F. Bake until dark golden brown, about 35 to 40 minutes. Cool thoroughly before slicing.

HONEY & CUMIN-GLAZED CORNISH HENS

Serves 8

The honey in this recipe symbolizes the hoped-for sweetness as the new year begins with this festive dish as its centerpiece.

GLAZE

½ cup honey
2 tablespoons fresh orange juice
2 tablespoons fresh lemon juice
2 tablespoons balsamic vinegar
3 tablespoons cumin seed, toasted and crushed
3 tablespoons olive oil
½ teaspoon salt
½ teaspoon freshly ground pepper

4 Cornish hens, split in half
Salt and pepper

COMBINE GLAZE INGREDIENTS. Preheat the oven to 400 degrees F. Rinse hens and blot dry. Sprinkle with salt and pepper. Using about a third of the glaze, brush both sides of hen halves. Place, skin side down, on a baking sheet with low sides. Place in oven and roast 10 minutes. Turn heat down to 375 degrees F., brush hens again with half the remaining glaze and roast 5 minutes. Turn hens over and roast 10 minutes. Brush with remaining glaze and roast until deep golden brown, about 5 minutes more. Let stand about 10 minutes before serving.

COUSCOUS WITH SAFFRON

AND VEGETABLES

The ruby glint of dried cranberries brightens this unusual dish of Sephardic inspiration. It may be served hot with the main course as a vegetable or at room temperature as a salad course or side dish.

2 cups chicken broth
½ cup water
¼ cup olive oil
¼ teaspoon saffron threads
½ teaspoon ground cinnamon
2 cups couscous
¾ cup dried cranberries or currants
2 medium zucchini, trimmed and diced
2 carrots, peeled and diced
Salt and pepper
3 scallions, sliced

13

IN A LARGE SAUCEPAN, BRING BROTH, WATER, OIL, SAFFRON, AND CINNAMON TO A BOIL. Gradually stir in the couscous. Cook, stirring until liquid is absorbed, about 2 minutes. Stir in cranberries, zucchini and carrots. Cover and let stand 15 minutes. Taste for salt and pepper and turn out into a serving bowl, breaking up lumps with your fingers. Sprinkle with scallions. Serve warm or at room temperature.

BRAISED APPLES AND RED CABBAGE

WITH WINE

Serves 8

This hearty vegetable side dish combines the honey and apples of the traditional Rosh Hashanah table.

2 tablespoons vegetable oil
1 large sweet onion, chopped
2 large apples, cored and chopped
2 tablespoons honey
1 large head red cabbage, cored and shredded
½ cup dry red wine
½ cup chicken broth or water
½ teaspoon salt
½ teaspoon freshly ground black pepper
¼ cup chopped parsley

IN A LARGE SKILLET, HEAT OIL. Cook onion and apples until very soft. Stir in honey and cook 1 minute. Add cabbage and cook until wilted. Add wine and broth or water. Bring to a boil, reduce heat, cover, and simmer until cabbage is tender, about 15 minutes. If mixture is too liquid, uncover and cook over high heat for a few minutes until some of the liquid evaporates. Stir in salt and pepper and serve sprinkled with parsley.

HANNAH'S HONEY CAKE

Serves 12

Cookies, cakes, honey-laced goodies, and sweets of many kinds recall the hope for sweet and joyful days ahead. Moist with coffee and apples, these almond-topped squares are a welcome reminder.

1 cup hot brewed coffee	1 teaspoon baking powder
1 teaspoon baking soda	1 teaspoon ground cinnamon
1 cup honey	1 teaspoon ground ginger
1 cup sugar	1 teaspoon freshly grated nutmeg
½ cup vegetable or canola oil	1 large apple, cored and grated
3 eggs	12 whole blanched almonds
3 cups all-purpose flour	

15

PREHEAT THE OVEN TO 350 DEGREES F. Grease a 9 x 13-inch baking pan. In a small bowl, combine coffee and baking soda. Set aside. In a large bowl, beat honey, sugar, and oil until well blended. Beat in eggs, one at a time, until mixture looks homogenized. In a medium bowl, sift together flour, baking powder, cinnamon, ginger, and nutmeg.

Beat flour mixture into honey mixture alternately with coffee mixture until well combined. Stir in apple. Pour batter into prepared pan. Place almonds on top of batter, to mark the center of each of 12 squares. Bake until golden brown, about 45 minutes. Cool and cut into squares.

YOM KIPPUR

THE MOST SOLEMN OF THE JEWISH HOLY DAYS, YOM KIPPUR IS A DAY OF

REFLECTION, ATONEMENT, AND COMPLETE FASTING. At the conclusion of

this day of worship and self-examination, friends and family come together to exchange

greetings and renew their strength. Foods served to break the fast are light and simple

restoratives, which usually include both salty and sweet dishes. ✷ This break-the-fast

menu is readied the day before; in fact, the flavors are enhanced by a day of melding.

It begins with soup, always welcome nourishment and comfort. Toasted or fresh bagels

are accompanied by an eggplant spread that is just savory enough after a day of fasting.

The easy-to-prepare almond dessert satisfies a natural craving for something sweet. Made

with pears, a fruit of the season, it is a moist cake that keeps exceptionally well.

FRESH VEGETABLE SOUP WITH

CHICKEN AND NOODLES

Serves 10 to 12

3 tablespoons vegetable oil
1 onion, chopped
1 leek, white part only, chopped
2 stalks celery, chopped
1 large carrot, diced
1 red bell pepper, seeded,
    deveined, and diced
1 small fennel bulb, chopped
½ head cabbage, shredded
4 plum tomatoes, seeded and
    coarsely chopped

2 zucchini, halved lengthwise
    and sliced
½ teaspoon dried oregano
¼ cup chopped parsley
6 cups chicken broth
3 cups water
8 ounces fine egg noodles
3 whole boneless and skinless
    chicken breasts, cut into strips
Salt and pepper

17

IN A LARGE POT, HEAT THE OIL. Cook onion, leek, celery, carrot, red pepper, fennel, and cabbage until barely tender, about 8 minutes. Stir in tomatoes, zucchini, oregano, and parsley. Cook until bubbly, about 2 minutes. Add broth and water and simmer 20 minutes. Add noodles and chicken and simmer 10 minutes.

Add salt and pepper to taste. Cool and refrigerate. Just before serving, reheat and taste again for salt. Serve hot.

TOASTED BAGELS WITH

EGGPLANT SPREAD

Serves 12

2 medium eggplants (about 2 pounds)
1 small onion, quartered
2 cloves garlic
½ cup parsley leaves
¼ cup basil leaves
1 small red pepper, roasted, peeled, and seeded
2 tablespoons tomato paste
3 tablespoons lemon juice
⅓ cup olive oil
⅛ teaspoon cayenne
Salt and pepper
12 bagels, halved and lightly toasted

18

PREHEAT THE OVEN TO 400 DEGREES F. Prick the skin of the eggplants and place on a baking sheet. Bake until eggplants collapse, about 45 minutes. Let cool completely.

Discard the stems from eggplants and cut into chunks. Place eggplants in a food processor with onion, garlic, parsley, basil, red pepper, tomato paste, lemon juice, olive oil, and cayenne. Process until a rough paste is formed. Taste and add salt and pepper. Spread on toasted bagel halves.

SPICED PEAR AND ALMOND CAKE

Serves 12

4 cups cored and coarsely chopped ripe pears (5 or 6 pears)
2 cups sugar
½ cup vegetable or canola oil
2 eggs, beaten
2 cups all-purpose flour
1 teaspoon ground cinnamon
½ teaspoon grated nutmeg
Grated zest of 1 lemon
2 teaspoons baking soda
½ teaspoon salt
1 teaspoon vanilla extract
1 cup chopped blanched almonds
Confectioners' sugar

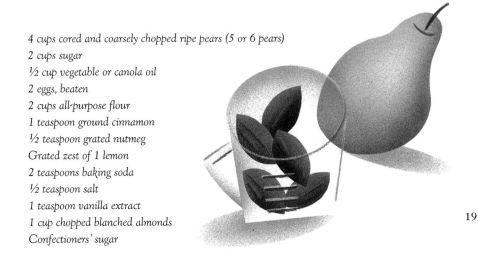

PREHEAT THE OVEN TO 350 DEGREES F. Grease a 10-inch round cake pan. Combine pears and sugar in a medium bowl and let stand 15 minutes. Combine oil with eggs and add to pears. In another bowl, combine flour, cinnamon, nutmeg, lemon zest, baking soda, and salt. Stir into pear mixture. Add vanilla and almonds. Pour into prepared pan and bake until cake tester inserted in center comes out clean, about 45 minutes. Cool on a rack about 20 minutes before turning out. Invert onto a serving platter and dust with confectioners' sugar.

SUCCOTH IS THE JEWISH THANKSGIVING. The weeklong festival begins on the fifth day after Yom Kippur and includes many joyous aspects, each with its own name. As *Hag ha'asif,* it is the Festival of the Harvest which coincides with the full moon and harvest time of ancient Palestine. It is also called *zeman simhatenu,* or Time of Rejoicing for the goodness and bounty of the earth. The word *succoth,* meaning booths, refers to the huts or temporary dwellings in which the Jews had to live in their 40 years wandering through the wilderness. ✷ The building of the *succah* is the most visible and dramatic aspect of this holiday and one which can involve the whole family. Children enjoy stringing cranberries and decorating the walls of the succah with autumn fruits and gourds. Everyone partakes of the excitement and novelty of eating the festival meals in the succah under its roof of boughs, which let the moon and stars shine through. ✷ Foods served during Succoth represent autumn and abundance partaken in a spirit of celebration and thanksgiving. The citron and palm branch (*etrog* and *lulav*), symbols of growing things, represent Succoth and figure prominently in the festival commemorations. This menu is meant as picnic fare which can be served outdoors at room temperature.

SWEET AND HOT PEPPER

TOMATO SOUP WITH MINT

Serves 8

Late-harvest sweet tomatoes and roasted red peppers lend their flaming colors to this piquant soup, which begins this picnic-fare menu with a burst of seasonal flavors.

2 tablespoons olive oil

6 ripe, fresh tomatoes or 4 cups canned tomatoes, seeded and chopped

3 red bell peppers, roasted, peeled, seeded, and chopped

3 cloves garlic, chopped

1 teaspoon ground cumin

¼ teaspoon harissa or ½ teaspoon hot pepper sauce or cayenne

1 tablespoon honey

1 cup tomato juice, vegetable stock, or water

1 tablespoon fresh lemon juice

Salt and pepper

¼ cup chopped mint leaves

IN A MEDIUM SAUCEPAN, HEAT OIL. Cook tomatoes and peppers on medium-high heat until mixture thickens, about 12 minutes. Stir in garlic, cumin, harissa, and honey. Simmer, uncovered, 10 minutes. Add tomato juice and puree in a blender or food processor. Stir in lemon juice. Add salt and pepper to taste. Serve at room temperature, hot, or chilled. Sprinkle with mint before serving.

PITA STUFFED WITH EGGPLANT SALAD

AND FETA CHEESE

Serves 8

Like a cornucopia, these pita halves spill over with the season's goodness, from herbed vegetables and briny olives to the irresistible pungency of feta cheese.

3 tablespoons olive oil

2 medium eggplants, cut into
    ½-inch cubes (about 1½ pounds)

1 large onion, chopped

2 cloves garlic, minced

2 cups seeded and chopped tomatoes,
    drained of liquid

2 tablespoons tomato paste

½ teaspoon dried oregano

½ teaspoon dried thyme

2 tablespoons balsamic or red wine vinegar

2 tablespoons capers, rinsed and drained

½ cup toasted walnuts, coarsely chopped

1 cup imported black olives, pitted and halved

¼ cup chopped parsley

4 ounces feta cheese, cut into small cubes

Salt and pepper

8 (6-inch) pita breads, halved and lightly toasted

IN A LARGE SKILLET, HEAT OIL. Sauté eggplants, onion, and garlic until slightly softened, about 5 minutes. Add tomatoes, tomato paste, oregano, thyme, and vinegar. Cook until bubbly and mixture thickens slightly, about 10 minutes. Remove from heat and stir in capers, walnuts, olives, and parsley. Let cool completely and gently toss with feta cheese. Add salt and pepper to taste. Stuff each pita half with eggplant salad.

Succoth

FENNEL, CUCUMBER, AND ORANGE SALAD

Serves 8

The orange in this salad takes the place of the traditional citron, a golden yellow, fragrant fruit that flourishes in Israel but is rarely available in the United States.

CITRUS VINAIGRETTE

½ teaspoon aniseed, crushed
3 tablespoons white wine vinegar
1 tablespoon fresh lemon juice
1 tablespoon fresh orange juice
4 tablespoons olive oil

_____

1 large hothouse cucumber, peeled, halved lengthwise, seeded, and sliced ¼-inch thick
2 medium fennel bulbs, cored, trimmed, and thinly sliced
2 oranges, peel and pith cut away, seeded, and thinly sliced
½ red onion, thinly sliced
¼ cup chopped parsley

WHISK TOGETHER VINAIGRETTE INGREDIENTS UNTIL WELL BLENDED. On a large shallow platter, arrange cucumber, fennel, oranges, and onion. Pour vinaigrette over salad and sprinkle with parsley.

BAKED FIGS WITH HONEYED YOGURT

Serves 8

This barely cooked dessert mixes an unexpected peppery punch with drizzles of honeyed yogurt. It makes a memorable conclusion to an out-of-doors dinner. There's something elegant about these petal-like figs, even if you do eat them with your hands—which is, after all, what everybody wants at a picnic.

16 fresh black figs
2 tablespoons canola oil
2 tablespoons freshly ground pepper (finely ground)
1 cup plain yogurt
1 tablespoon fresh lemon juice
3 tablespoons honey

25

PREHEAT THE OVEN TO 400 DEGREES F. Lightly brush figs with oil. Sprinkle each fig with pepper. Place upright on an oiled baking sheet and bake until darkened and soft, about 12 minutes. Meanwhile, combine yogurt with lemon juice and honey.

With kitchen scissors, cut a deep X on top of each fig. Figs will appear to have 4 petals. Place 2 figs on each plate and drizzle with honeyed yogurt. Serve warm or at room temperature.

THE STORY OF HANUKKAH IS THE SAGA OF A PEOPLE'S TRIUMPH OVER THREATENED ANNIHILATION. When the Maccabees recaptured the Temple of Jerusalem, they discovered that there was sufficient oil for only one day. Miraculously, however, the precious oil lasted for eight full days and nights. Hanukkah, then, is a celebration of survival, of the preservation of identity, as elementary as the conquest of good over evil. ✳ Hanukkah is the only one of the major Jewish holidays not recounted in the Bible, and much of its symbolism is open to interpretation. Was Hanukkah, as some say, originally a recognition of the solstice? Did it become a family-based holiday and de-emphasize its military connotation because Jews living under the Romans realized the imprudence of celebrating victory over a powerful ruler? Do we eat foods fried in oil to commemorate those rekindled flames from Jerusalem? Does the word *latkes* come from the Greek word for oil (*elaion*)? Are latkes symbols of the hastily made food the Maccabees ate prior to going to battle? Does the *dreidel*–a spinning top–signify a game that Jews, who were reading the Torah, pretended to be playing when they were caught by watchful oppressors? Is Hanukkah *gelt*–gold foil-covered chocolate coins–symbolic of the coins the Hasmoneans minted upon achieving independence? ✳ Hanukkah will always be full of such puzzles and wonderments. And there will always be as many opinions as there are latkes recipes. Certainly there is nothing like a latkes party for exchanging and explaining traditions and passing them along to the next generation.

27

SPINACH SALAD WITH TANGERINES

AND DRIED CRANBERRIES

Serves 8

In the age-old spirit of Jewish cooking, this salad uses the foods of the season. It may be a prelude to the array of fried pancakes that follow or a refreshing palate-cleanser between courses.

1 cup dried cranberries

8 cups fresh spinach, washed, stemmed, and torn into bite-size
     pieces (about 1 pound)

3 seedless tangerines, peeled, pith removed, and sectioned

1 cup toasted pecans, coarsely chopped

DRESSING

3 tablespoons sherry vinegar

2 tablespoons cranberry soaking water

½ cup peanut or vegetable oil

⅛ teaspoon freshly grated nutmeg

¼ teaspoon freshly ground black pepper

½ teaspoon salt

SOAK CRANBERRIES IN 2 CUPS HOT WATER UNTIL SOFT, ABOUT 1 HOUR. Drain, discarding all but 2 tablespoons of soaking liquid. Reserve liquid and cranberries separately.

In a large bowl, combine cranberries, spinach, tangerines, and pecans. In a medium bowl, whisk together dressing ingredients until well combined. Toss with spinach mixture and serve.

28

LATKES

While latkes are synonymous with Hanukkah for Eastern European Jews, they are unknown to Jews of other cultures. Greek Jews make honey-dipped fried sweets called loukomades or boumuelos. In Israel, the jam-filled, deep-fried sufganiyot is the tradition, while Persian Jews enjoy zelebi as the important holiday sweet.

"Designer latkes"–that's what some people call anything other than potato latkes. In fact, the Jewish Community Center near us recently held a Latkes Contest and strongly encouraged the creation of wildly innovative latkes recipes. After several weeks of waiting for entries, however, they had to cancel the event because nobody signed up!

CLASSIC POTATO LATKES

Makes about 16

1 ½ pounds all-purpose potatoes, peeled
1 medium onion, chopped or grated
¼ cup chopped parsley (optional)
1 egg, lightly beaten
3 tablespoons all-purpose flour
1 teaspoon salt
¼ teaspoon freshly ground black pepper
½ to 1 cup oil, for frying
Apple sauce, for serving
Sour cream, for serving

30

GRATE POTATOES AND SQUEEZE OUT AS MUCH MOISTURE AS YOU CAN. Combine with onion, parsley, egg, flour, salt, and pepper. Heat about ⅓ cup oil in a large frying pan over medium-high heat, until very hot. Drop about 2 tablespoons mixture into pan to form each pancake. Use the back of a spoon to flatten mixture so that each latke is about 3 inches in diameter. Fry until brown and crisp, about 4 minutes per side. Drain on paper towels and keep warm in a 250 degree F. oven. This will have to be done in batches. Use more oil as needed for each batch. Serve hot with apple sauce and/or sour cream.

ZUCCHINI LATKES

Makes about 16

4 cups coarsely grated zucchini (about 2 pounds)
1 small onion, chopped or grated
1 egg, lightly beaten
¼ cup grated parmesan cheese
¼ cup heavy cream
¼ cup all-purpose flour
1 teaspoon baking powder
½ teaspoon salt
⅛ teaspoon cayenne
½ teaspoon dried oregano
½ to 1 cup oil, for frying
Parmesan cheese for serving (optional)

SQUEEZE OUT AS MUCH MOISTURE AS POSSIBLE FROM ZUCCHINI AND COMBINE WITH REMAINING INGREDIENTS EXCEPT OIL. In a large frying pan over medium-high heat, heat about ⅓ cup oil until hot. Drop 3 tablespoons zucchini mixture into pan to form each pancake. Fry until golden brown, about 4 minutes per side. Drain on paper towels and keep warm in a 250 F. degree oven. Serve with a sprinkling of parmesan cheese, if desired.

FRESH SALMON LATKES

Makes about 15

1 ½ pounds boneless and skinless salmon fillet
1 small onion
1 stalk celery
3 sprigs parsley
2 tablespoons chopped fresh dill
½ teaspoon salt
⅛ teaspoon cayenne
1 tablespoon fresh lemon juice
1 egg
1 egg white
1 ½ cups dry bread crumbs
½ to 1 cup oil, for frying
Tartar sauce, for serving (optional)

CUT SALMON INTO CHUNKS AND PLACE IN FOOD PROCESSOR WITH ONION, CELERY, PARS-
LEY, DILL, SALT, AND CAYENNE. Process until chopped but not pureed. Add lemon juice,
egg, egg white, and ½ cup of the bread crumbs and process again, just until combined.
Measure out about ¼ cup salmon mixture for each latke and form into 3-inch patties.
Spread remaining bread crumbs on a plate and coat both sides of each latke with them.

In a large frying pan over medium-high heat, heat about ⅓ cup oil. Fry latkes until gold-
en brown, about 4 minutes per side. Use more oil for each batch as needed. Drain on
paper towels and keep warm in a 250 degree F. oven until ready to serve. Serve as soon
as all are done. Serve with tartar sauce, if desired.

CAULIFLOWER AND CARROT LATKES

4 cups cauliflower florets (about 1 large head)

2 eggs, lightly beaten

½ cup all-purpose flour

½ teaspoon baking powder

½ teaspoon ground cumin

½ teaspoon ground coriander

½ teaspoon salt

¼ teaspoon freshly ground black pepper

1 large carrot, peeled and grated

½ to 1 cup oil for frying

33

COOK CAULIFLOWER IN LARGE POT OF SALTED BOILING WATER UNTIL TENDER, ABOUT 12 MINUTES. Drain and let cool. Puree cauliflower with eggs and stir in remaining ingredients except oil.

In a large frying pan over medium-high heat, heat about ½ cup oil until hot. Ladle 3 tablespoons batter into pan to form each pancake. Fry until golden, about 3 minutes per side. Use more oil as needed for each batch. Drain on paper towels and keep warm in a 250 degree F. oven. Serve as soon as all are done.

SWEET COTTAGE CHEESE LATKES

Makes about 16

Dairy foods are important at Hanukkah. Some trace the custom to the story of Judith, whose delicious cheesecakes so distracted the Assyrian general Holofernes that she was able to behead him, thus saving the Jews from slaughter.

> 1 cup regular or lowfat cottage cheese
> 3 eggs, separated
> 1 cup all-purpose flour
> 2 tablespoons sugar
> ½ cup heavy cream
> Pinch salt
> Grated zest of ½ lemon
> ½ cup oil, for frying
> Apple-Pear Puree (recipe follows)

BEAT COTTAGE CHEESE, EGG YOLKS, FLOUR, SUGAR, CREAM, SALT, AND LEMON ZEST UNTIL SMOOTH. Beat egg whites until stiff but not dry and fold into cheese mixture.

In a large frying pan over medium-high heat, heat oil until hot. Drop 4 tablespoons batter into the pan to form each latke. Fry until golden, about 4 minutes per side. Use more oil for each batch as needed. Drain on paper towels and keep warm in a 250 degree F. oven until ready to serve. Serve with Apple-Pear Puree.

Apple-Pear Puree

3 ripe Comice or Anjou pears, peeled, cored, and quartered
3 Golden Delicious apples, peeled, cored, and quartered
¼ cup water
2 tablespoons fresh lemon juice
½ cup sugar, or to taste

PLACE ALL INGREDIENTS IN A HEAVY SAUCEPAN. Cover and cook over medium-low heat until fruit is soft and starts to break down, 12 to 14 minutes. Uncover and cook over medium-high heat until mixture thickens, about 5 minutes. Puree in a food mill or food processor. Serve warm or at room temperature.

35

PURIM IS A JOYFUL HOLIDAY, A SPECIAL FAVORITE OF CHILDREN
WITH A SWEET TOOTH. The last holiday before Passover, it is a time to use
up the last of the flour in the house by making baked goods and special treats.
Children not only delight in eating these goodies, they also enjoy delivering them
to friends and neighbors in the Purim tradition of *shalah manot*. In this custom of
sharing, which fulfills the biblical command of "sending portions one to another,"
one family sends a food gift, usually a platter of baked goods and fruit, to another.
That family repays the kindness, contributes additional food gifts and sends the
platter on. Traditionally children are the willing messengers for these happy
transfers. ✳ The seasonal nature of these customs has led some scholars to
speculate that they were originally part of an end-of-winter feast, a hopeful
turning to the life-affirming stirrings of spring. The holiday is tied to the biblical
story of the evil Haman, minister to the Persian King Ahasuerus, who takes
offense with the Jew Mordecai, a relative of the king's wife, Queen Esther. Haman
persuades the king to issue an edict to kill Mordecai along with all the Jews in
the kingdom. Esther bravely reveals to the king that she is a Jew and persuades
him to rescind the order, thus saving her people. King Ahasuerus then has Haman

killed in the gallows intended for Mordecai. The word *purim,* or lots, refers to the fact that Haman cast lots to determine the date for the extermination of the Jews. ✳ Instead of a day of mourning, Purim, or 14 Adar, is a celebration of life and survival. The most carnival-like of Jewish holidays, it is characterized, in various parts of the world, by the wearing of masks and costumes, by masquerade parties and dancing, a festive *seudah,* or banquet, and a special spirit of gaiety (*ad lo yadah*) that makes everyone look forward to its arrival. ✳ Purim also marks the founding of the Women's National Zionist Organization in 1912 by Henrietta Szold. She named the group Hadassah, which means Esther in Hebrew, in honor of the heroine of the Purim story.

38

HAMANTASHEN

No one seems to be able to resolve the question of the symbolism of these triangular filled cookies. Are haman-tashen modeled after Haman's three-cornered hat, or his pocket? Do they represent Abraham, Isaac, and Jacob? Or do they relate to the words Tash kocho, meaning "May Haman's strength become weak"? More easily resolved is the dilemma about which kind to make—the child's preferred cookie-dough hamantashen or the adult's yeast-dough version. We hereby provide one of each: the former inspired by the all-time child-favorite Fig Newtons; the latter, an almondy, fruit-filled pastry.

HAMANTASHEN WITH PRUNE FILLING

Makes about 24

DOUGH

1 package dry yeast
1 ¼ cups warm water (about 110 degrees F.)
½ cup sugar
8 tablespoons (1 stick) unsalted butter or margarine,
    melted and cooled
½ teaspoon salt
2 eggs, beaten
About 4 cups all-purpose flour

FILLING

1 pound pitted prunes, chopped
4 tablespoons water
1 tablespoon fresh lemon juice
¼ cup honey
2 teaspoons grated lemon zest
⅓ cup almonds, ground in food processor

STIR YEAST INTO ¼ CUP OF THE WATER ALONG WITH 3 TABLESPOONS OF THE SUGAR.
Let stand until foamy on surface, about 4 minutes. In a large mixing bowl, combine
the remaining water, remaining sugar, butter or margarine, salt, eggs, and yeast mixture.
Stir in flour gradually until a soft dough is formed. Turn dough out onto a floured
surface and knead about 3 minutes. If sticky, add more flour. Form dough into a ball

and place in a greased bowl. Cover and place in a warm spot, until doubled in bulk, about 1 hour.

Meanwhile make filling. Cook prunes in water over low heat, about 10 minutes. Add lemon juice and honey and cook another 5 minutes. Mixture should be fairly thick. Add lemon zest and almonds, stirring well to combine. Let cool.

Punch down dough and let rest about 5 minutes. Roll out ⅛ inch thick. Cut circles with a 4-inch cookie cutter. Place about 2 teaspoons prune filling in center of each circle. Pinch edges of the dough together, leaving a small opening in center. The pastry will be in the shape of a triangle, with a small amount of filling showing through center. Place on greased cookie sheets, cover, and let rise about 1 hour.

Preheat the oven to 375 degrees F. Examine hamantashen before putting in oven and pinch seams again if they seem to be opening. Bake until golden brown, about 20 minutes. Let cool on rack 10 minutes before removing.

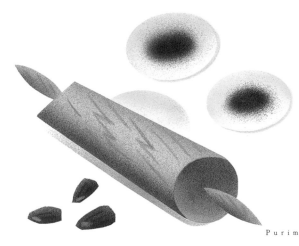

HAMANTASHEN WITH FIG FILLING

Makes about 24

DOUGH

¾ cup sugar

2 cups all-purpose flour

2 teaspoons baking powder

¼ teaspoon salt

8 tablespoons unsalted butter
   or margarine (1 stick),
   cut into small pieces

1 egg, lightly beaten

3 tablespoons fresh orange juice

FILLING

¼ pound dried figs, chopped

½ cup water

1 teaspoon fresh lemon juice

42

COMBINE SUGAR, FLOUR, BAKING POWDER, AND SALT IN A FOOD PROCESSOR. Pulse in butter or margarine until mixture resembles cornmeal. Add egg and orange juice and process just until dough forms. Form into 8-inch disk, wrap in plastic, and refrigerate 2 hours or overnight.

Combine filling ingredients in a saucepan and cook over medium heat until most of the liquid evaporates, about 10 minutes. Let cool and puree in a food processor.

Preheat the oven to 400 degrees F. Line cookie sheets with parchment paper or grease them. On a floured surface, roll out dough ⅛-inch thick. Cut into circles with a 3-inch cookie cutter. Place 1 teaspoon filling in center of each circle. Pinch 3 edges of dough together, leaving a small opening in center for filling to peek through. The pastry will be a triangle with a little filling showing. Place on prepared cookie sheets and bake until golden brown, about 20 minutes. Let cool on rack 10 minutes before removing.

WALNUT AND DRIED CHERRY RUGELACH

Makes 32

Pitted dried cherries make for easy assembly of these little gems. They get their flaky texture from a light cottage-cheese dough.

DOUGH

2 cups all-purpose flour
½ pound (2 sticks) unsalted butter
    or margarine, cut into small
    pieces, at room temperature
½ pound whole milk cottage cheese
Pinch salt

FILLING

½ cup cherry jam, whisked until smooth
½ cup chopped walnuts
½ cup chopped pitted dried cherries

————————

2 tablespoons sugar
1 teaspoon ground cinnamon

43

IN A FOOD PROCESSOR OR MIXER, COMBINE DOUGH INGREDIENTS UNTIL A SMOOTH DOUGH FORMS. Divide into 4 pieces and form each into a 5-inch disk. Wrap in plastic and refrigerate 3 hours or overnight.

Preheat the oven to 375 degrees F. On a lightly floured surface, roll out each disk to an 8-inch circle, ⅛-inch thick. Spread each circle with 2 tablespoons of jam. Sprinkle with ¼ of the walnuts and ¼ of the cherries. With a pastry wheel or a sharp knife, cut each circle into 8 wedges. Starting at outside edge, roll up each wedge to enclose filling. Place, point side down, on greased cookie sheet. Combine sugar and cinnamon and sprinkle each pastry with mixture. Bake until golden brown, about 35 minutes. Place on cooling rack and let pastries rest 10 minutes before removing from cookie sheet.

APRICOT-ALMOND-CHOCOLATE BALLS

Makes about 48

These sugar-dusted chocolates can be served as either candy or cookies, at teatime, after dinner, or as a perfect accompaniment to the wines of Purim. Children especially enjoy rolling up the dough into little balls, which need no cooking once assembled.

½ pound dried apricots
½ pound almonds, toasted
2 ounces bittersweet chocolate, cut into small pieces
1 cup sugar
8 tablespoons water
Confectioners' sugar

44

PLACE APRICOTS, ALMONDS, AND CHOCOLATE IN A FOOD PROCESSOR AND PROCESS UNTIL VERY FINELY CHOPPED. In a medium saucepan over medium-high heat, cook sugar and water until soft ball stage, about 240 degrees F. on a candy thermometer, about 10 minutes. Stir in apricot mixture and let cool. Squeeze mixture together with hands to make a firm ball. Pinch off about 1 tablespoon of mixture at a time, form into 1-inch balls, and roll in powdered sugar. Place in paper candy cups and serve.

CHOCOLATE-ORANGE SQUARES

Makes 9

These chocolate squares are wonderful with the wine, which figures prominently at Purim, recalling the "banquet of wine" that Queen Esther prepared leading to Haman's downfall. The Talmud directs that one drink wine until one "does not know" (ad lo yadah) the difference between Mordecai and Haman.

8 tablespoons (1 stick) unsalted
   butter or margarine
2 ounces unsweetened chocolate,
   cut into small pieces
1 ounce bittersweet chocolate,
   cut into small pieces
2 eggs
½ cup sugar
½ cup orange marmalade
½ teaspoon vanilla extract
⅔ cup all-purpose flour

½ teaspoon baking powder
¼ teaspoon salt

GLAZE

3 tablespoons unsalted butter or margarine
3 ounces bittersweet chocolate, cut into small pieces
1 tablespoon corn syrup
_____

Grated zest of 1 orange

45

PREHEAT THE OVEN TO 350 DEGREES F. Grease a 9-inch square cake pan. In a medium saucepan over low heat, melt butter or margarine with chocolate. Pour into a mixing bowl and let cool about 10 minutes. Add eggs, sugar, and marmalade to chocolate mixture and whisk until smooth. Stir in vanilla, flour, baking powder, and salt just until flour disappears. Pour into prepared pan and bake until surface is shiny, about 30 minutes. Remove to cooling rack and let rest until cool.

For the glaze, melt butter with chocolate and stir in corn syrup. Spread cake with glaze and sprinkle with orange zest. Let glaze set until fairly firm, then cut into 3-inch squares.

WHAT MAKES THIS NIGHT DIFFERENT FROM ALL OTHER NIGHTS?

This is the question the youngest child asks to begin the Pesach, or Passover, Seder. Ask this question of any cook who has lovingly labored over this Jewish holiday meal and you will receive a response with a different perspective. Since during Passover foods may not be prepared with any flour, grains, grain products, or leavening agents, there is no bread, no pasta, no rice, no pastries made with flour. For most Jews, corn, beans, lentils, and their by-products are prohibited as well, although Sephardic Jews allow rice and beans to be eaten during Passover. The Passover Seder is also a night of heavy-duty eating, a multicourse meal that must represent traditions of the past yet be tempered with dishes suited for today's lifestyle. ✴ For these reasons, Passover can be a challenge to anyone planning the Passover Seder, with its detailed and specific directions for food preparation and serving. (The word *Seder*, after all, means order.) And yet, perhaps no meal or holiday conjures up such fond memories as does Passover, as our talks with grandmothers and great-grandmothers revealed. From one, we heard about Miriam. ✴ "Boiled carp was a fresh-water fish my mother used to get from the fishmonger. Usually for gefilte fish she used a mix of carp and white fish. But once my mother bought a live carp from the fishmonger and filled the bathtub with water and put it in. We came home from school, and we were delighted. We were throwing bread crumbs to it. It was a pet. And we gave the fish a name. We called it Miriam. And then Friday we came from school and we made our usual beeline for the bathroom but Miriam was gone. We ran into the kitchen. Mama, what happened to Miriam? 'What do you mean what happened to Miriam. I made the gefilte fish!' We were so upset. 'You killed Miriam!' we said. You think anyone would eat that fish?" ✳ Another cook tells of the annual appearance of her bag of potato starch, which she takes down from the high shelf for Passover desserts. "It makes any cake lighter and finer," she explains. "I don't know why I don't use it year round. For some reason, I just don't think of it." ✳ And there is always talk of *matzo brei* ("If you want to be fancy, you can serve it with applesauce.") And of *noant*, which one cook recalls that her mother made with boiled black radishes and honey; another remembers her mother using walnuts. As for the prune-filled pastry called *chremsel*, one woman in her eighties says she has to make them every year for her brother "because the only time he had them was when my mother made them. He even takes some home. He eats them the next day cold." And also with chremsel we get another lesson: "Chremsel is singular; if you make a lot you're making *chremslach*." ✳ As told in the Book of Exodus, the story of Passover is a journey of freedom. At the Passover table, through the ritual of food and reading of the Haggadah, or recital, the participants acknowledge and celebrate the meaning and implications of that freedom. It is indeed a different night, but the best part of it is perhaps that so much remains the same.

48

CARROT-MATZO BALL SOUP

Matzo balls have been called the only truly authentic Jewish dish, since all other Jewish foods have eastern European, Sephardic, or other national roots. Our version tends toward the lightness school of matzo-ball construction.

MATZO BALLS

4 eggs

4 tablespoons melted chicken fat, margarine or vegetable oil

½ cup chicken broth or water

1 cup matzo meal

½ teaspoon salt

½ teaspoon freshly ground black pepper

3 tablespoons chopped fresh dill

1 medium carrot, peeled and finely grated

———————

4 quarts chicken broth

IN A LARGE BOWL, BEAT EGGS WITH CHICKEN FAT AND BROTH UNTIL WELL BLENDED. Stir in remaining ingredients for matzo balls. Refrigerate about 1 hour.

Bring a large pot of salted water to a boil. With wet hands, gently form matzo balls about 1½ inches in diameter. You should have about 28 balls. Do not make them compact. Slip into boiling water. When they come to the surface, turn water down to a bare simmer, cover, and cook about 35 minutes. Remove with slotted spoon. Refrigerate if not using in the next hour or so.

Heat chicken broth with matzo balls. Serve soup with 3 or 4 matzo balls per person.

49

ROLLED TURKEY BREAST WITH

MUSHROOM-SPINACH STUFFING

Serves 10 to 12

Even at the liveliest Passover Seder, slices of this juicy turkey breast, with its swirls of spinach-green stuffing, never fail to stop the conversation. Although the dish takes a bit of preparation, it is not at all difficult and the results are overwhelmingly gratifying to both cook and guests.

STUFFING

2 tablespoons oil or chicken fat
2 leeks, white parts only, chopped
1 pound mushrooms, chopped
2 cloves garlic, minced
1 tablespoon dried tarragon
6 cups chopped fresh spinach (6 ounces)
1 tablespoon fresh lemon juice
About 1½ cups matzo meal
Salt and pepper

TURKEY

1 whole kosher turkey breast, boned with skin left on (4 to 5 pounds)
Salt and pepper
3 tablespoons kosher-for-Passover mustard
1 tablespoon oil
2 cups chicken broth
½ cup kosher-for-Passover dry white wine

50

IN A LARGE SKILLET OVER MEDIUM-HIGH HEAT, HEAT OIL. Cook leeks and mushrooms until leeks are tender and mushrooms brown, about 10 minutes. Stir in garlic, tarragon, and spinach. Cook just until spinach wilts, about 2 minutes. Remove spinach mixture to a large bowl and let cool slightly. Sprinkle with lemon juice and stir in matzo meal. Taste and add salt and pepper.

Lay the turkey breast, skin side down, in front of you. Starting at the center and holding a knife parallel to the meat with the blade facing left, make a lengthwise cut into the meat. Open the flap. Repeat on the right side. Spread the meat out flat and cover with wax paper. Pound until about ¾-inch thick. Sprinkle with salt and pepper. Spread with 2 tablespoons of the mustard and then with the stuffing, leaving a ½-inch border all the way around. Starting at left or right, roll the breast into a cylinder. Tie at 1-inch intervals with kitchen string and secure open edges with toothpicks.

Preheat the oven to 350 degrees F. Place turkey on a rack, seam side down, in a roasting pan. Brush with oil. Combine 1 cup of the broth with wine and pour some over the turkey. Roast about 1 hour, basting with stock mixture every 15 minutes until done. Internal temperature should be 150 degrees F. and juices should run clear. Remove from oven and let turkey rest at least 20 minutes before slicing.

Skim fat from roasting pan. Pour pan juices into a small saucepan with remaining stock and remaining mustard. Cook until slightly thickened. Remove toothpicks and string from turkey and cut into 1-inch slices. Pass sauce separately.

ASPARAGUS WITH ORANGE VINAIGRETTE

Serves 8 to 10

Passover is the feast of springtime, and perhaps nothing proclaims the new and hopeful season so eloquently as fresh asparagus. With a splash of dressing and a sprinkling of chopped olives, this citrusy combination is equally welcome as either salad or vegetable.

3 pounds asparagus, trimmed and peeled

ORANGE VINAIGRETTE

2 tablespoons kosher-for-Passover white wine vinegar
1 tablespoon fresh lemon juice
2 tablespoons fresh orange juice
1 tablespoon kosher-for-Passover mustard
1 teaspoon honey
Grated zest of ½ orange
½ cup olive or vegetable oil
Salt and pepper

¼ cup chopped black olives

COOK ASPARAGUS IN A LARGE POT OF BOILING WATER, JUST UNTIL TENDER, ABOUT 3 TO 4 MINUTES. Drain and cool under cold water. Place asparagus on cooling racks lined with paper towels. Set aside.

Combine vinaigrette ingredients until well blended. Taste for salt and pepper. Just before serving, arrange asparagus on serving platter. Drizzle with dressing and sprinkle with olives.

DRIED CHERRY AND PEAR HAROSET

Makes about 2 cups

There are endless recipes for haroset, which symbolizes the bricks and mortar from which the Israelites were forced to build the pyramids while in slavery to the Pharaoh. But haroset is also sweet, as in contrast to the bitter herbs of enslavement, and as a reminder of the sweet hope of freedom. This ginger-spiked version of haroset makes use of dried cherries, which have recently become widely available. As a family project, this recipe, with its dicing and grating and slicing, gives everyone something to do. Its rich fruit flavors have their roots in Sephardic traditions.

½ cup dried pitted cherries
½ cup diced dried pears
1 cup walnut pieces
2 fresh pears, peeled, cored, and cut into small pieces
½ teaspoon fresh lemon juice
½ teaspoon ground cinnamon
1 teaspoon freshly grated gingerroot
2 tablespoons sugar, or to taste
½ cup kosher-for-Passover sweet red wine

PROCESS INGREDIENTS IN A FOOD PROCESSOR UNTIL A ROUGH PASTE IS FORMED. Taste and adjust sugar if necessary. Spread on matzo or use as a relish.

SWEET-POTATO KUGEL

Kugels come in many types—noodle, potato, fruit, even matzo meal—but they are all essentially baked puddings. Any golden-brown kugel is always welcome, and this is a particularly pretty one that gets its sunny color from sweet potatoes. It makes a delicious accompaniment to the turkey breast or to any roasted or broiled chicken dish.

6 medium sweet potatoes, preferably Garnet or Jewel,
    peeled and grated (about 2 ½ pounds)
1 large onion, finely chopped
½ cup minced chives (optional)
2 eggs, lightly beaten
¼ cup potato starch
¼ cup matzo meal
½ teaspoon salt
½ teaspoon freshly ground black pepper
¼ cup melted chicken fat or oil

54

PREHEAT THE OVEN TO 375 DEGREES F. Grease a 9 x 13-inch baking pan. Combine all ingredients until well blended. Pour batter into prepared baking dish. Bake until golden brown, about 1 hour. Let cool and cut into 12 squares.

PASSOVER BISCOTTI

Based on Italian Jewish versions of biscotti, these spectacular almond slices substitute matzo cake meal and potato starch for flour. They are so good we make them year round.

1 cup ground almonds
½ cup kosher-for-Passover potato starch
½ cup matzo cake meal
¾ cup sugar
1 teaspoon kosher-for-Passover baking powder
Grated zest of ½ lemon
3 eggs, lightly beaten
Juice of ½ lemon
1 cup coarsely chopped blanched almonds

55

PREHEAT THE OVEN TO 300 DEGREES F. Line a cookie sheet with parchment paper. In a food processor, process ground almonds, potato starch, matzo cake meal, sugar, and baking powder and zest until blended. Add eggs and lemon juice and process just until dough holds together. Turn out onto a board dusted with cake meal and knead chopped almonds into dough. Dough should be slightly tacky to the touch but not wet. Form dough into 2 logs about 2 inches in diameter. Place on cookie sheet. Flatten slightly with wet hands.

Bake until golden brown, about 50 minutes. Remove from oven and place logs on cutting board. Slice on the diagonal, about 1 inch thick. Return slices, cut side down, to cookie sheet. Bake until golden brown, about 45 minutes. Cool on a rack. Store in an airtight container.

SHAVUOTH

SHAVUOTH, OR WEEKS, IS KNOWN BY SEVERAL NAMES. It is called Pentecost and the Feast of Weeks because it falls on the fiftieth day after the second night of Passover. This locates Shavuoth in the midst of spring, when the earth is beginning to yield to the season's warm proddings. Shavuoth is thus called *Hag Ha-bikurim*, the Feast of the First Fruits, to bring to mind one of the three pilgrimages from Palestine to the Temple of Jerusalem, where the products of the harvest were presented in offering. ✷ On Shavuoth, God's covenant with Israel on Mount Sinai as told in the Book of Exodus is also commemorated. This makes Shavuoth *Zeman Matan Toratenu*, or the Season of the Giving of the Torah, and it is sometimes marked by children's confirmation ceremonies or the registering of children in Hebrew class. This commitment is reflected in the story of Ruth which is read on Shavuoth and contains the inspiring words "Whither thou goest, I will go; . . . thy people shall be my people, and thy God, my God." (Ruth I:16). ✷ This joy-filled two-day holiday (one day among Reform Jews and in Israel) is made even more festive by decorating with greenery and plants and enjoying the good foods of the season. Preparing dairy-based dishes is sometimes traced to the custom of serving morning refreshments to those who have studied the Torah all night on Shavuoth. The prospect of cheese blintzes and latkes, noodle pudding, and cheesecakes makes it a much anticipated celebration.

COLD BEET AND CUCUMBER SOUP

Serves 6

Diced cucumbers and beets make this soup a tasty introduction to this early summer holiday meal.

> 6 cups vegetable broth or water
> 5 medium beets, trimmed, peeled, and quartered
> 1 large cucumber, preferably hothouse, peeled and seeded
> 1 cup sour cream or yogurt
> 3 tablespoons finely chopped mint leaves
> Salt and pepper
> 6 sprigs mint, for garnish

BRING BROTH OR WATER TO A BOIL. Add beets and simmer, partially covered, until beets are tender, about 30 minutes. Remove 6 pieces of beet. Cut into small dice and set aside. Puree remaining beets with cooking liquid and ½ cucumber. Dice remaining cucumber and set aside. Stir sour cream into puree until well blended. Stir in diced beets and cucumbers. Refrigerate until well chilled, about 4 hours or overnight.

Just before serving, stir in the chopped mint and taste for salt and pepper. Ladle into bowls, garnish each with a sprig of mint, and serve.

ASPARAGUS AND HERBED CHEESE STRUDEL

Serves 10

This flaky golden strudel may look complicated, but when the recipe is done in stages, it becomes a simple assembly job. Besides, the delighted look on people's faces as they take the first taste is worth the little fuss involved.

1 pound thin asparagus, trimmed
    and cut into 1-inch pieces
4 ounces mild goat cheese
4 ounces cream cheese
2 tablespoons chopped fresh tarragon
    or 1 teaspoon dried tarragon

2 tablespoons chopped chives
¼ teaspoon salt
½ teaspoon freshly ground black pepper
8 sheets phyllo dough, at room temperature
¼ cup melted butter

COOK ASPARAGUS ABOUT 3 MINUTES IN BOILING SALTED WATER. Drain and rinse under cold water. Set aside to cool on a rack lined with paper towels.

Preheat the oven to 375 degrees F. Grease a baking sheet. Combine cheeses with tarragon, chives, salt, and pepper until smooth. Stir in cooked asparagus pieces.

Place a sheet of phyllo dough horizontally in front of you. Brush with butter. Continue until you have a stack of 4 sheets. Do not brush top sheet with butter. Using half the filling, spread an even 3-inch-wide strip about 1 inch from the bottom and 2 inches from the sides. Fold up the bottom and fold in the sides of the dough and roll up like a jelly roll. Place the strudel, seam side down, on the baking sheet. Brush top and sides with butter. With a sharp knife, cut several slits in top of strudel. Repeat with remaining phyllo sheets and filling.

Bake until golden brown and crispy, about 30 minutes. Let cool about 15 minutes before serving. Cut 3-inch-thick slices with a serrated knife.

POACHED SALMON WITH TWO SAUCES

Serves 8

Everybody loves this elaborate-looking presentation, especially the cook since everything can be prepared one or two days in advance. Served at room temperature, it is perfect for any warm-weather occasion.

> *2 cups dry white wine*
> *4 cups water*
> *2 tablespoons fresh lemon juice*
> *1 teaspoon salt*
> *4 parsley sprigs*
> *1 bay leaf*
> *1 scallion*
> *8 salmon steaks, about 1 inch thick (about 6 ounces each)*
> *Lemon Mustard Sauce (recipe follows)*
> *Roasted Tomato and Red Pepper Sauce (recipe follows)*

COMBINE WINE, WATER, LEMON JUICE, SALT, PARSLEY, BAY LEAF, AND SCALLION IN A SKILLET LARGE ENOUGH TO HOLD SALMON IN 1 LAYER. (Or divide between 2 skillets.) Bring to a boil over high heat and gently place salmon in the liquid. Reduce heat so that liquid is at a bare simmer. Cover and cook 3 minutes. Remove from heat and uncover. Let salmon cool in poaching liquid. Serve at room temperature or refrigerate up to 1 day and bring to room temperature before serving. Pass both sauces with salmon.

Lemon-Mustard Sauce

½ cup mayonnaise
½ cup yogurt or sour cream
1 tablespoon grated lemon zest
2 tablespoons fresh lemon juice
2 teaspoons Dijon mustard
2 tablespoon chopped fresh dill
Salt and pepper

WHISK TOGETHER ALL INGREDIENTS UNTIL WELL BLENDED. Taste for salt and pepper. May be made 1 day ahead and refrigerated. Bring to room temperature before serving.

Roasted Tomato and Red Pepper Sauce

61

4 large tomatoes, roasted, peeled, and seeded
1 large red bell pepper, roasted, peeled, and seeded
1 clove garlic
½ sweet onion, peeled and cut into small pieces
½ teaspoon crushed red pepper
2 tablespoons fresh lemon juice
1 teaspoon sugar
3 tablespoons olive oil
salt and pepper
¼ cup chopped cilantro

PLACE ALL INGREDIENTS EXCEPT CILANTRO IN A BLENDER OR FOOD PROCESSOR AND BLEND UNTIL SMOOTH. Taste for salt and pepper and stir in cilantro. May be made 1 day ahead and refrigerated. Bring to room temperature before serving.

VERY BERRY BLINTZES

Serves 8

This fresh berries dish is always a treat and a particularly good choice for shehehiyanu, *the blessing over the new fruits of the season.*

BATTER

2 eggs
½ teaspoon salt
1 cup water
1 cup all-purpose flour
Butter or oil, for frying

FILLING

8 ounces regular milk or lowfat cottage cheese, drained
8 ounces cream cheese
Pinch salt
¼ cup sugar
1 egg yolk
1 teaspoon grated lemon zest
1 cup blueberries or raspberries or a combination

Berry Sauce (recipe follows)

WHISK TOGETHER EGGS, SALT, AND WATER UNTIL WELL BLENDED. Whisk in flour, a little at a time, until batter is smooth. Let stand about 30 minutes.

Heat a small amount of butter or oil in a well seasoned or nonstick 6- or 7-inch skillet. Make sure pan is very hot. Pour about 3 tablespoons batter into pan, tilting it so that batter covers bottom of pan evenly. Cook about 2 to 3 minutes. Uncooked side will lose its shine and look dull when ready. Remove and repeat process until all the batter is used. Stack blintz rounds one on top of another. You should have at least twelve.

With electric beater, combine cottage and cream cheese with salt, sugar, egg yolk, and lemon zest. Fold berries in by hand. Place about 2 tablespoons filling in center of cooked side of blintz. Fold 2 opposite sides over filling, then overlap the other 2 sides. Repeat with remaining blintzes, and filling.

In a large skillet over medium-high heat, heat butter or oil. Place filled blintzes in pan, seam side down. Cook until golden brown, about 3 minutes per side. Serve 1 or 2 blintzes per person with a spoonful of berry sauce poured over each.

Makes about 1½ cups

Berry Sauce

1 pint strawberries, hulled and halved
¼ cup seedless raspberry jam
1 tablespoon fresh lemon juice
¼ to ½ cup confectioners' sugar

PUREE INGREDIENTS IN A BLENDER OR FOOD PROCESSOR.

FOODS OF THE SABBATH

OF ALL THE JEWISH HOLY DAYS, THE SABBATH IS THE OLDEST AND THE ONLY ONE SPECIFICALLY REFERRED TO IN THE TEN COMMANDMENTS. From the Hebrew word *shabbat,* to rest, the Sabbath is a time to spend with the family in peace, celebration, and festivity. It begins at sundown on Friday with the lighting of the candles and blessing of the braided challah, traditionally covered with an embroidered cloth, and ends at sun-down Saturday with the *Havdalah,* or separation of the Sabbath from the rest of the week. The fragrance of mixed spices, including cloves and nutmeg, represents the hope for a sweet week ahead. ✴ A custom perhaps as old as the Sabbath itself calls for inviting an *oyreah,* or stranger, to dinner to share the meal with the family so that no one is left alone on this warm and welcoming occasion. *Shabbat shalom,* a peaceful Sabbath, is the greeting of the day. ✴ Except for challah, Sabbath foods vary according to nationality and tradition; this menu, like the Sabbath, welcomes a variety of influences.

GOLDEN CHALLAH BREAD

Makes 2 loaves

On the Sabbath, the two braided loaves of challah symbolize the double portion of manna gathered on the eve of the Sabbath during the Exodus. Even the embroidered cloths are symbolic, representing the dew which covered the manna. After the hamotzi, the thanksgiving for the bread which begins the Sabbath, each person receives a portion of challah. Traditionally, no one speaks until after the bread has been tasted.

2 recipes challah, without raisins (page 11)

MAKE THE DOUGH AS DIRECTED ON PAGE 11. After punching dough down, knead dough and divide in half. Cover 1 half and divide other into three. Roll each piece, with your hands, into a rope 12 inches long. Braid 3 ropes together and pinch ends to seal. Repeat with other half. Continue as directed on page 11.

TOMATO AND ONION BRAISED BRISKET

Serves 8

This is a hearty and delicious, make-ahead feast-in-a-pot and a wonderfully warming focal point for the Sabbath meal.

> 1 piece brisket (4 to 5 pounds)
> Salt and pepper
> ½ teaspoon dried oregano
> ½ teaspoon dried thyme
> 2 cloves garlic, minced
> ¼ cup olive oil
> 2 large onions, thinly sliced
> 2 cups coarsely chopped tomatoes

TRIM ALMOST ALL OF THE EXCESS FAT FROM BRISKET AND SPRINKLE WITH SALT AND PEPPER. Make a paste of the oregano, thyme, garlic, and olive oil. Spread over both sides of brisket. Let stand at room temperature for 1 hour.

Preheat the oven to 300 degrees F. Place brisket in a roasting pan. Cover with onions and then with tomatoes. Cover pan tightly with foil. Bake 3½ to 4 hours, basting every hour with accumulated juices. Remove brisket and tomato mixture to a platter. Degrease pan juices and pour over meat. Refrigerate overnight for easy slicing. Slice and reheat with tomato mixture and pan juices and serve.

ROASTED GARLIC POTATO WEDGES

Serves 8

Most potato dishes garner a universal audience, but these start attracting fans as soon as their garlicky fragrance begins escaping from the oven.

6 baking potatoes, scrubbed
3 tablespoons olive oil
2 cloves garlic, minced
½ teaspoon salt
1 teaspoon Hungarian sweet paprika

PREHEAT THE OVEN TO 425 DEGREES F. Cut each potato lengthwise into 6 wedges. Place in a bowl. Combine oil, garlic, salt, and paprika and toss with potatoes, coating them thoroughly with mixture. Place potatoes in a single layer on a greased baking sheet. Bake until potatoes are golden brown and tender, about 20 to 25 minutes. Serve hot.

68

SUGAR SNAP PEAS AND

HONEYED CARROTS

Serves 8

This bright mix of color and taste can serve as a vegetable dish or appetite-provoking first course.

4 large carrots, cut into matchsticks
½ cup chicken broth or water
⅛ teaspoon cayenne
½ pound sugar snap peas, cut into strips
2 tablespoons honey
2 tablespoons fresh orange juice
2 tablespoons fresh lemon juice
Salt and pepper
¼ cup chopped chives

IN A LARGE SKILLET BRING CARROTS AND BROTH TO A BOIL. Cover and cook 1 minute. Remove cover and add cayenne and peas. Cook until almost all liquid has evaporated. Stir in honey, orange juice, and lemon juice. Cook another 3 minutes. Taste for salt and pepper. Sprinkle with chives and serve.

STRAWBERRY, PINEAPPLE, AND
MANGO COMPOTE

Serves 8

The tropical touch of toasted coconut and mango adds a bit of excitement to this refreshing mélange.

MANGO SAUCE

1 large mango, peeled and seeded
2 tablespoons fresh lemon juice
3 tablespoons honey
1 tablespoon dark rum

2 pints strawberries, hulled and quartered
1 small pineapple, peeled, cored, and cut into 1-inch pieces
1 small mango, peeled and cut into 1-inch pieces
1 cup shredded coconut, toasted

IN A FOOD PROCESSOR OR BLENDER, PUREE THE MANGO WITH LEMON JUICE, HONEY, AND RUM. Set aside.

Place strawberries, pineapple, and mango in a large bowl. Toss with mango sauce. Sprinkle with toasted coconut and serve.

Index

Apricot-Almond-Chocolate Balls, 44

Asparagus and Herbed Cheese Strudel, 59

Asparagus with Orange Vinaigrette, 52

Baked Figs with Honeyed Yogurt, 25

Braised Apples and Red Cabbage
with Wine, 14

Carrot-Matzo Ball Soup, 49

Chocolate-Orange Squares, 45

Cold Beet and Cucumber Soup, 58

Couscous with Saffron and Vegetables, 13

Dried Cherry and Pear Haroset, 53

Fennel, Cucumber, and Orange Salad, 24

Fresh Vegetable Soup with
Chicken and Noodles, 17

Golden Challah Bread, 66

Hamantashen

Hamantashen with Fig Filling, 42

Hamantashen with Prune Filling, 40

Hannah's Honey Cake, 15

Honey & Cumin-Glazed Cornish Hens, 12

Latkes

Cauliflower and Carrot Latkes, 33

Classic Potato Latkes, 30

Fresh Salmon Latkes, 32

Sweet Cottage Cheese Latkes, 34

Zucchini Latkes, 31

Passover Biscotti, 55

Persimmon and Pomegranate Salad, 10

Pita Stuffed with Eggplant Salad and
Feta Cheese, 23

Poached Salmon with Two Sauces, 60

Roasted Garlic Potato Wedges, 68

Rolled Turkey Breast with Mushroom-
Spinach Stuffing, 50

Round Raisin Challah, 11

Spiced Pear and Almond Cake, 19

Spinach Salad with Tangerines and
Dried Cranberries, 28

Strawberry, Pineapple, and Mango
Compote, 70

Sugar Snap Peas and Honeyed Carrots, 69

Sweet and Hot Pepper Tomato Soup
with Mint, 22

Sweet-Potato Kugel, 54

Toasted Bagels with Eggplant Spread, 18

Tomato and Onion Braised Brisket, 67

Very Berry Blintzes, 62

Walnut and Dried Cherry Rugelach, 43

Table of Equivalents

Length Measures

⅛ in	3 mm
¼ in	6 mm
½ in	12 mm
1 in	2.5 cm
2 in	5 cm
3 in	7.5 cm
4 in	10 cm
5 in	13 cm
6 in	15 cm
7 in	18 cm
8 in	20 cm
9 in	23 cm
10 in	25 cm
11 in	28 cm

Liquids

US	Metric	UK
2 tbl	30 ml	1 fl oz
¼ cup	60 ml	2 fl oz
⅓ cup	80 ml	3 fl oz
½ cup	125 ml	4 fl oz
⅔ cup	160 ml	5 fl oz
¾ cup	180 ml	6 fl oz
1 cup	250 ml	8 fl oz
1½ cups	375 ml	12 fl oz
2 cups	1 l	32 fl oz

Weights

US/UK	Metric
1 oz	30 g
2 oz	60 g
3 oz	90 g
4 oz (¼ lb)	125 g
5 oz (⅓ lb)	155 g
6 oz	185 g
7 oz	220 g
8 oz (½ lb)	250 g
10 oz	315 g
12 oz (¾ lb)	375 g
14 oz	440 g
16 oz (1 lb)	500 g
1½ lb	750 g
2 lb	1 kg
3 lb	1.5 kg

Oven Temperatures

Fahrenheit	Celsius	Gas
250	120	½
275	140	1
300	150	2
325	160	3
350	180	4
375	190	5
400	200	6
425	220	7
450	230	8
475	240	9
500	260	10

The exact equivalents in the preceding tables have been rounded for convenience.